This book belongs to:

....

____

AVA PLANTS A SEED

Laura Boden

Ava woke up one morning with an exciting thought in her head.

She threw on some clothes
and **welly boots...**

...then ran down to the garden **shed**.

"I'm going to grow something in a **pot** from just a single **seed!**" thought Ava.

"But **where** do I start?...
What do I plant?...
Do I have **everything** I need?"

In the shed were **pots** and **soil**.
Equipment that Ava will need.

A **watering can, tools** and **gloves**.
Drawers full of **bulbs** and **seeds**.

DAISY
POPPY
GRASS
SEEDS

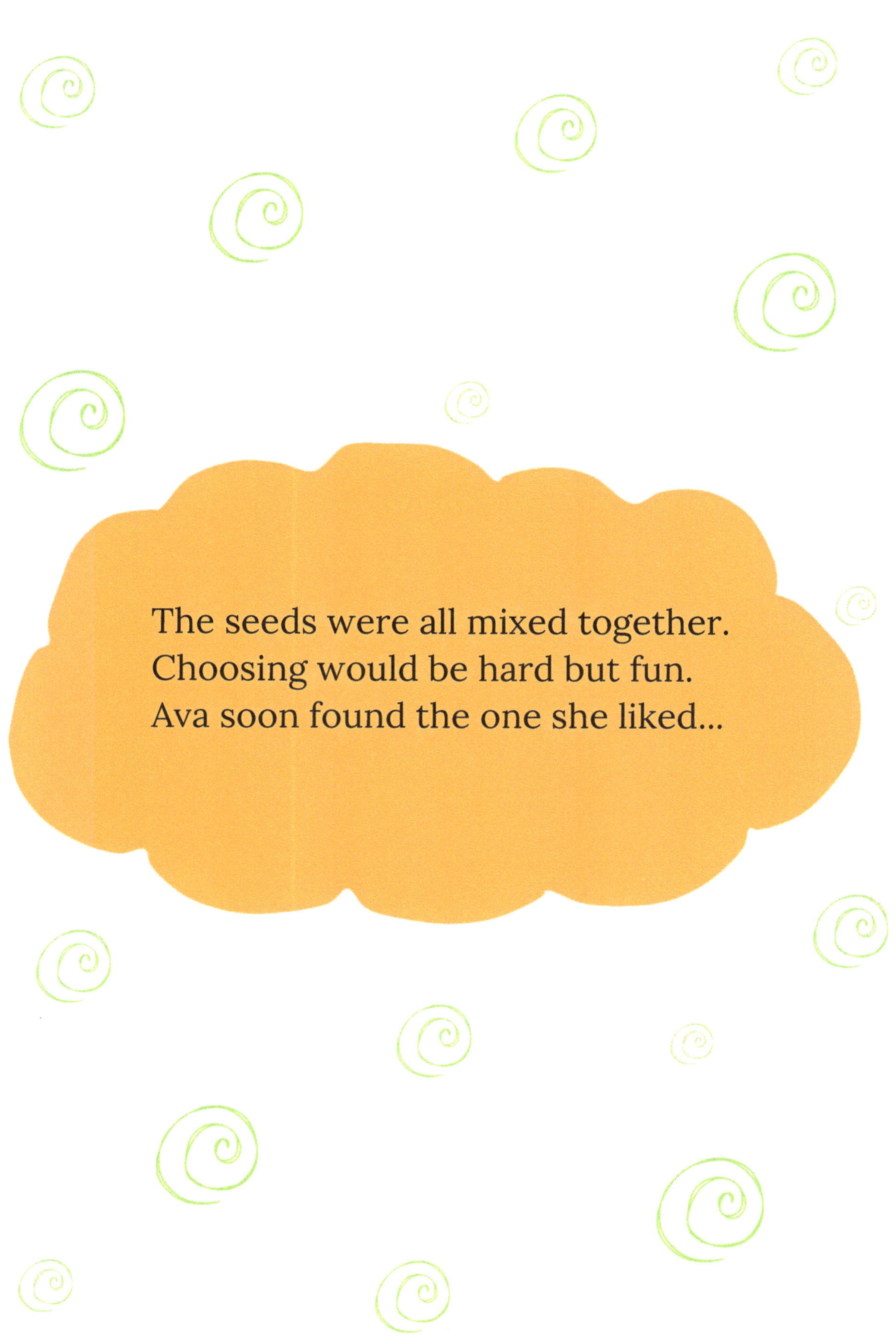

The seeds were all mixed together.
Choosing would be hard but fun.
Ava soon found the one she liked…

...and it was the **biggest one!**

She took large scoops of **compost**
and filled up a brown plastic **pot.**

Made a finger hole right in the middle, big enough for the **seed** to be dropped.

With her chosen seed now **planted** and
the **pot** carefully placed on the **shelf**...

...Ava hoped the **sunlight** would also
be of some help.

Everyday Ava would visit;
Waiting for something to show!
But Ava had **no idea**...

...the growing stage would be so **very slow!**

Each time she sprinkled it with **water**.

Watching and waiting eagerly.

February

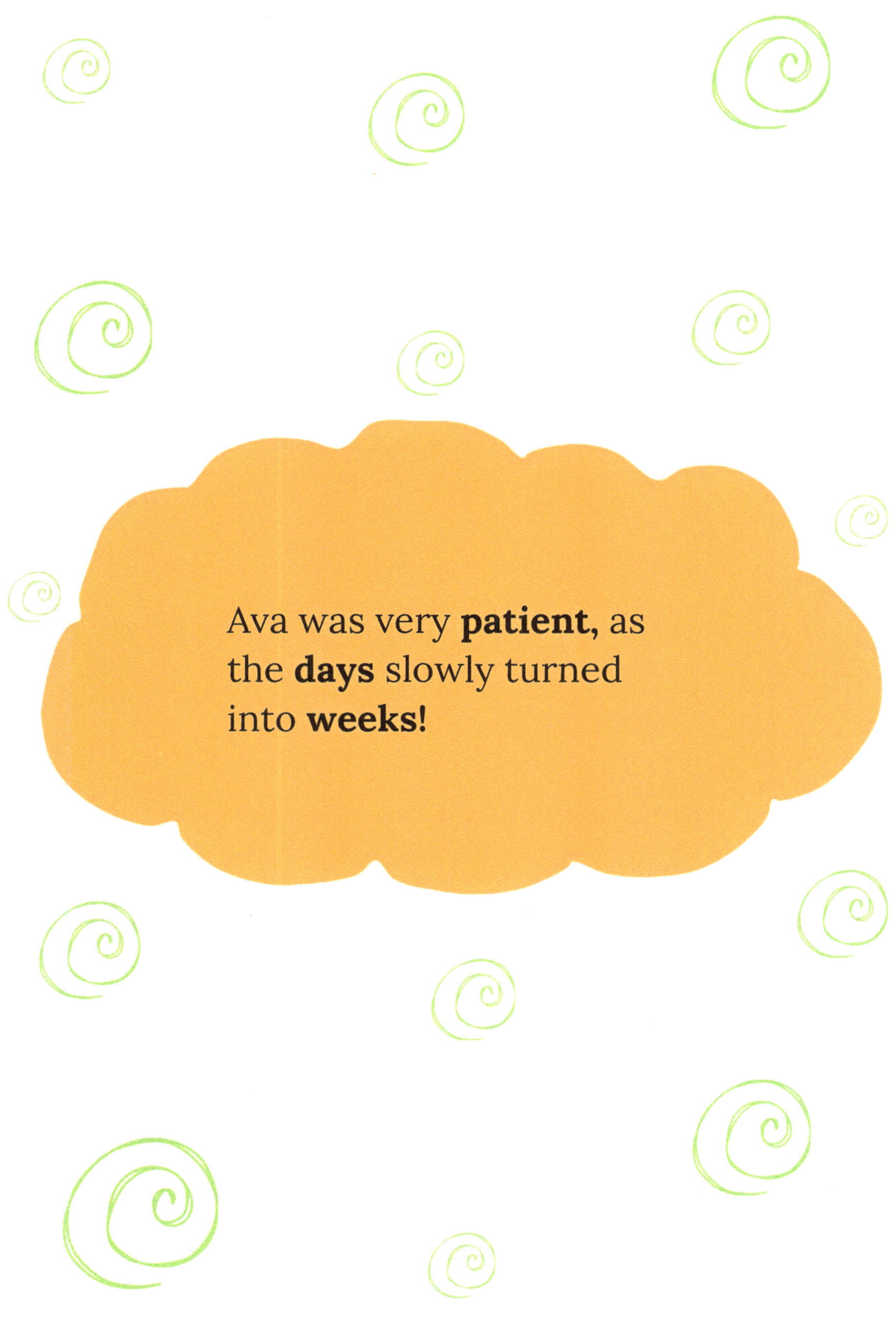

Ava was very **patient,** as the **days** slowly turned into **weeks!**

Suddenly, one morning a
shoot had appeared!
Sprouting three beautiful,
green **leaves**!

She showed her parents the **seedling**.
Ava asked, "What **plant** will it be?"

Her parents looked at each other then said,
"Ava, that's not a **plant** it's a **tree!**"

Ava was **so** excited.

She told **all** her friends at school.

They all started planting their
own little **seeds.**

They thought it was *awfully cool!*

The children were very excited.
Hoping their **seedlings** would grow
big and tall...

...for the ones that grew the strongest, would be planted all around the school!

Ava's seed was now
a tall **sapling** and
needing a new home
to be found...

They cleared a large space
in the **garden**...

...and **planted** it snug in the **ground**.

Everyday Ava would visit. Watching it **grow** more **branches** and **leaves**.

Ava often dreamt about it growing
into a **huge** Oak Tree.

"I wonder just **how big** it will get!" Ava thought.

"As now it's
Bigger than ME!"

Glossary

Bulb Part of the plant, under the soil, that stores food while the plant is resting.

Branch Part of a tree which grows out from the trunk.

Compost Brown, decomposed material that is full of nutrients. Perfect for planting or improving soil.

Garden A piece of ground or space where flowers, plants, shrubs, trees and vegetables can be grown.

Leaves Part of a plant attached to the stem that collects sunlight. The sunlight is turned into energy (food).

Plant Living thing that grows in the ground or from seeds and bulbs in a pot. They have a stem, leaves, branches and can flower.

Pot A rounded container used for growing seeds and plants.

Seed Part of a seed plant enclosed in a seed coat which can grow into a plant.

Seedling A young plant grown from seed.

Shed A small, outdoor building where things are stored.

Shoot First part of a plant that appears above soil level that has a stem, leaves and buds.

Sapling A young tree.

Wordsearch

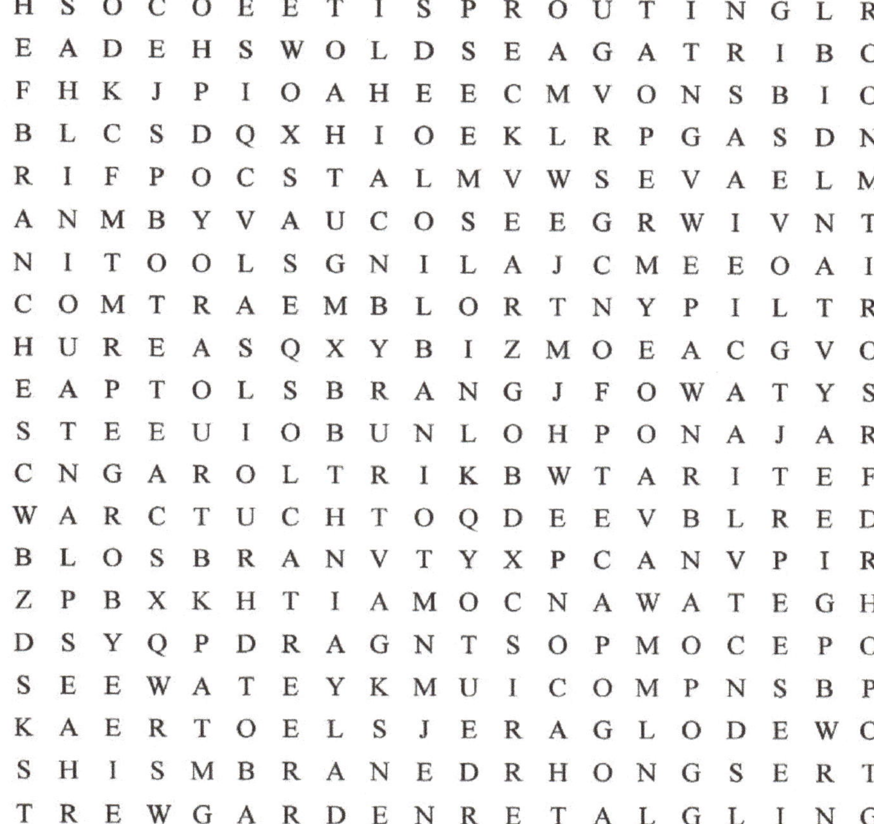

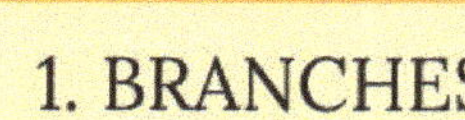

1. BRANCHES	9. SEED
2. BULB	10. SHED
3. COMPOST	11. SPROUTING
4. GARDEN	12. SUNLIGHT
5. GLOVES	13. TOOLS
6. LEAVES	14. TREE
7. POT	15. WATER
8. PLANT	16. WELLY BOOTS

For all children who love nature.
Enjoy growing something of your very ow. - L.B.